Let this serve as a catalyst
for creativity, self-expression, and artistic exploration,
while also celebrating the rich symbolism and imagery
of the tarot tradition

1

THE FOOL'S DILEMMA

PROMPT

Illustrate the duality of life, the balance between opposites.

The Fool symbolizes both the positive aspects of innocence, fearlessness, and optimism, as well as the negative traits of naivety, recklessness, and irresponsibility. It represents a fresh start, unlimited potential, and a willingness to take risks, but also warns against being careless or oblivious to potential dangers.

2

THE MAGICIAN

PROMPT

Depict a modern interpretation of the Magician.

The Magician represents manifestation, power, and resourcefulness. It symbolizes the ability to channel energy and resources to create desired outcomes. The Magician reminds us of our potential to shape our reality through focus, willpower, and creativity. It encourages us to harness our skills and talents to achieve our goals and manifest our intentions into reality.

3

THE HIGH PRIESTESS

PROMPT

Create an artwork inspired by the mysteries and intuition of the High Priestess.

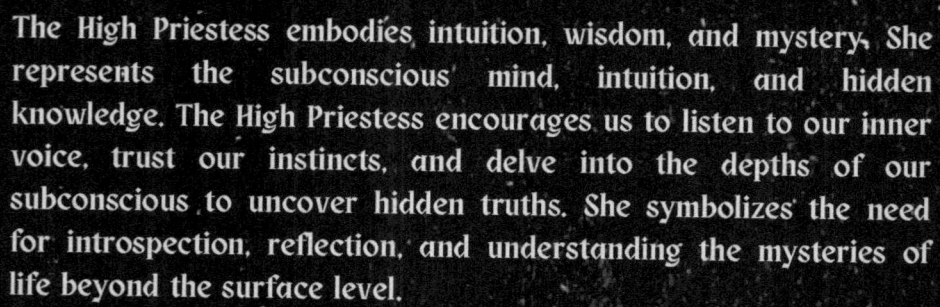

The High Priestess embodies intuition, wisdom, and mystery. She represents the subconscious mind, intuition, and hidden knowledge. The High Priestess encourages us to listen to our inner voice, trust our instincts, and delve into the depths of our subconscious to uncover hidden truths. She symbolizes the need for introspection, reflection, and understanding the mysteries of life beyond the surface level.

4

THE EMPRESS

PROMPT

Illustrate abundance, fertility, and motherhood in the style of the Empress.

The Empress represents femininity, nurturing, and abundance. She symbolizes fertility, creativity, and motherhood. The Empress encourages us to connect with our nurturing side, embrace abundance in all its forms, and cultivate creativity in our lives. She signifies the beauty of nature, the importance of self-care, and the power of creation and growth.

5

THE EMPEROR

PROMPT

Explore themes of authority, structure, and leadership in your artwork.

The Emperor represents authority, stability, and structure. He embodies the qualities of leadership, discipline, and control. The Emperor encourages us to establish order in our lives, set clear boundaries, and take responsibility for our actions. He symbolizes the need for structure and organization to achieve our goals and maintain stability in our endeavors.

THE HIEROPHANT

PROMPT

Create a piece that symbolizes tradition, spirituality, or religious beliefs.

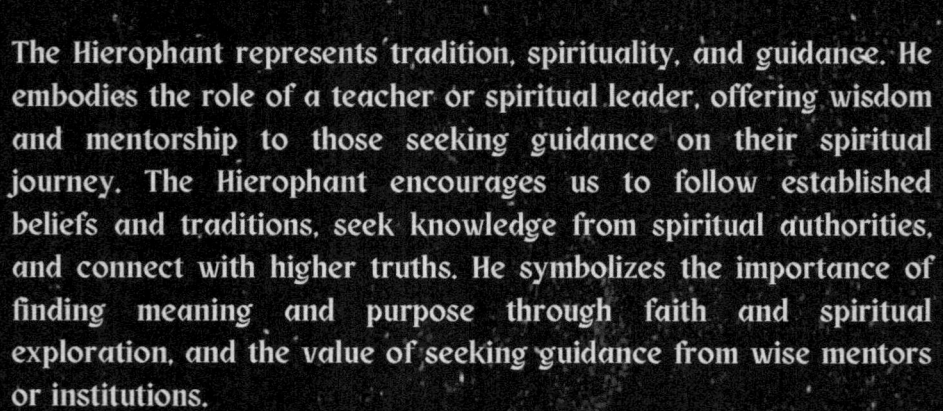

The Hierophant represents tradition, spirituality, and guidance. He embodies the role of a teacher or spiritual leader, offering wisdom and mentorship to those seeking guidance on their spiritual journey. The Hierophant encourages us to follow established beliefs and traditions, seek knowledge from spiritual authorities, and connect with higher truths. He symbolizes the importance of finding meaning and purpose through faith and spiritual exploration, and the value of seeking guidance from wise mentors or institutions.

7

THE LOVERS

PROMPT

Depict love, partnership, and harmony in your artwork.

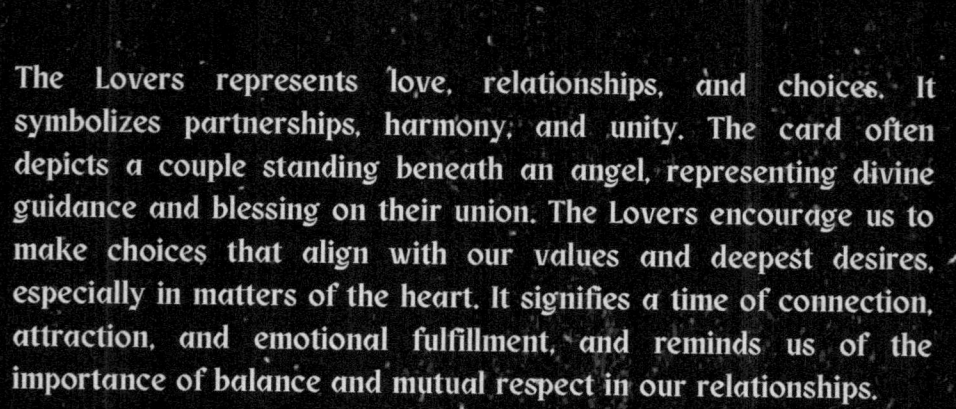

The Lovers represents love, relationships, and choices. It symbolizes partnerships, harmony, and unity. The card often depicts a couple standing beneath an angel, representing divine guidance and blessing on their union. The Lovers encourage us to make choices that align with our values and deepest desires, especially in matters of the heart. It signifies a time of connection, attraction, and emotional fulfillment, and reminds us of the importance of balance and mutual respect in our relationships.

8

THE CHARIOT

PROMPT

Illustrate determination, willpower, and victory
in the style of the Chariot.

The Chariot represents determination, willpower, and control. It symbolizes victory, triumph, and overcoming obstacles through focused effort and perseverance. The card often depicts a charioteer driving forward with confidence, guiding two opposing forces or energies in harmony. The Chariot encourages us to harness our inner strength, stay focused on our goals, and navigate life's challenges with courage and determination, ultimately leading to success and achievement.

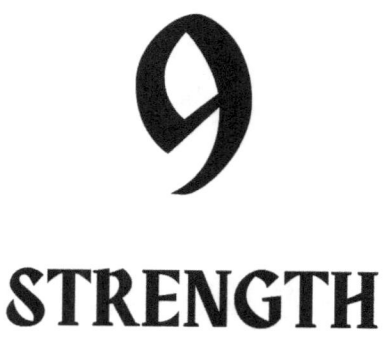

STRENGTH

PROMPT

Create an artwork that embodies inner strength, courage, and resilience.

The Strength represents inner strength, courage, and resilience. It symbolizes the ability to overcome challenges with grace and compassion rather than force. The card often depicts a woman gently taming a lion, illustrating the power of gentleness and inner calm to conquer adversity. Strength encourages us to face our fears, tap into our inner reserves of courage and compassion, and embrace our vulnerabilities as sources of strength. It reminds us that true strength comes from within and enables us to endure and triumph over life's difficulties.

10

THE HERMIT

PROMPT

Explore themes of introspection, solitude, and inner guidance.

The Hermit represents introspection, solitude, and wisdom. It symbolizes a period of inner reflection, seeking answers within oneself rather than from external sources. The card often depicts a lone figure holding a lantern, suggesting the illumination of inner truth and enlightenment. The Hermit encourages us to withdraw from distractions, take time for introspection, and seek guidance from our inner wisdom. It signifies a journey of self-discovery, introspection, and spiritual enlightenment, leading to a deeper understanding of oneself and the world.

11

WHEEL OF FORTUNE

PROMPT

Depict the cyclical nature of life, fate, and destiny in your artwork.

The Wheel of Fortune signifies the cycles of life, destiny, and change. It reminds us that life is unpredictable, with ups and downs, and encourages us to adapt to change and embrace new opportunities as they arise.

12

JUSTICE

PROMPT

Illustrate themes of balance, fairness, and truth.

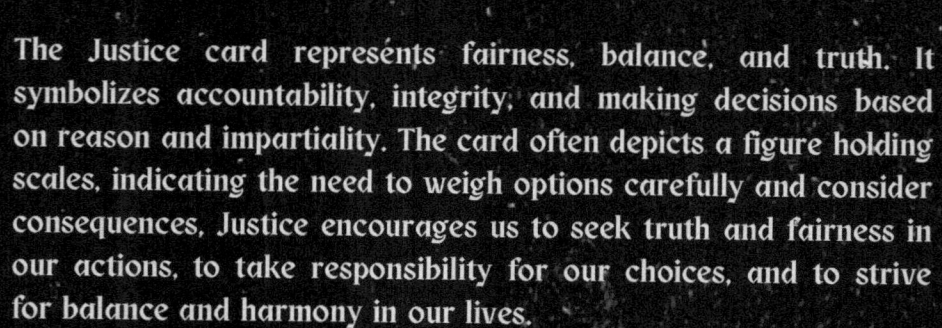

The Justice card represents fairness, balance, and truth. It symbolizes accountability, integrity, and making decisions based on reason and impartiality. The card often depicts a figure holding scales, indicating the need to weigh options carefully and consider consequences. Justice encourages us to seek truth and fairness in our actions, to take responsibility for our choices, and to strive for balance and harmony in our lives.

13

THE HANGED MAN

PROMPT

Create an artwork that explores surrender, sacrifice, and new perspectives.

The Hanged Man represents suspension, surrender, and perspective shift. It symbolizes sacrifice and letting go of control to gain new insights and understanding. It often depicts a figure hanging upside down, suggesting a different perspective and a willingness to see things from a new angle. The Hanged Man encourages us to release attachments, surrender to the present moment, and embrace a period of introspection and spiritual growth.

14

DEATH

PROMPT

Depict transformation, endings, and new beginnings in your artwork.

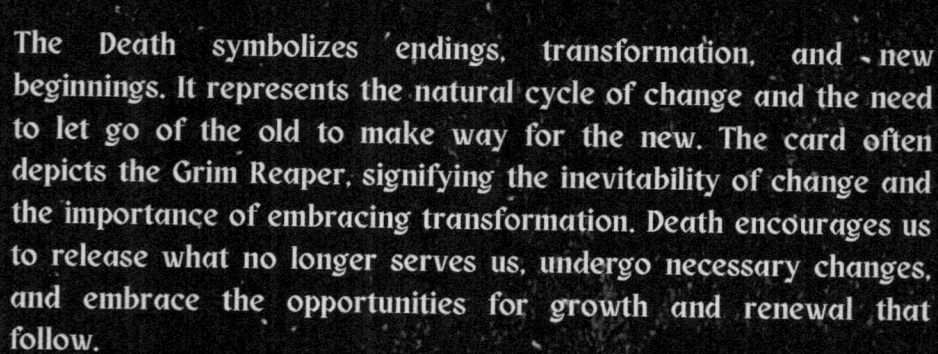

The Death symbolizes endings, transformation, and new beginnings. It represents the natural cycle of change and the need to let go of the old to make way for the new. The card often depicts the Grim Reaper, signifying the inevitability of change and the importance of embracing transformation. Death encourages us to release what no longer serves us, undergo necessary changes, and embrace the opportunities for growth and renewal that follow.

15
TEMPERANCE

PROMPT

Explore themes of moderation, balance, and harmony in your artwork.

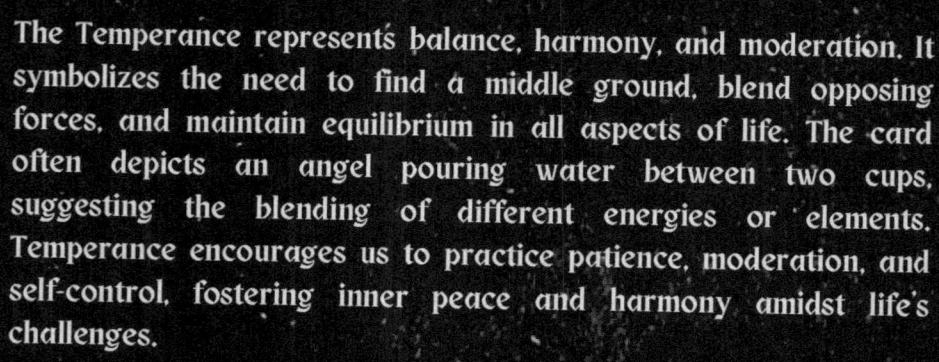

The Temperance represents balance, harmony, and moderation. It symbolizes the need to find a middle ground, blend opposing forces, and maintain equilibrium in all aspects of life. The card often depicts an angel pouring water between two cups, suggesting the blending of different energies or elements. Temperance encourages us to practice patience, moderation, and self-control, fostering inner peace and harmony amidst life's challenges.

16

THE DEVIL

PROMPT

Illustrate themes of bondage, temptation, or materialism.

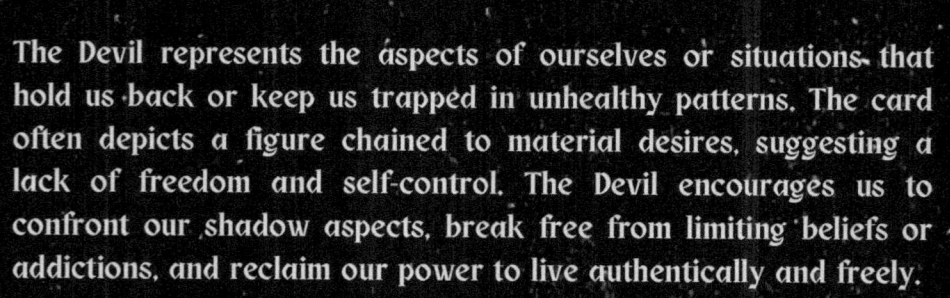

The Devil represents the aspects of ourselves or situations that hold us back or keep us trapped in unhealthy patterns. The card often depicts a figure chained to material desires, suggesting a lack of freedom and self-control. The Devil encourages us to confront our shadow aspects, break free from limiting beliefs or addictions, and reclaim our power to live authentically and freely.

17

THE TOWER

PROMPT

Depict sudden change, upheaval, and revelation in your artwork.

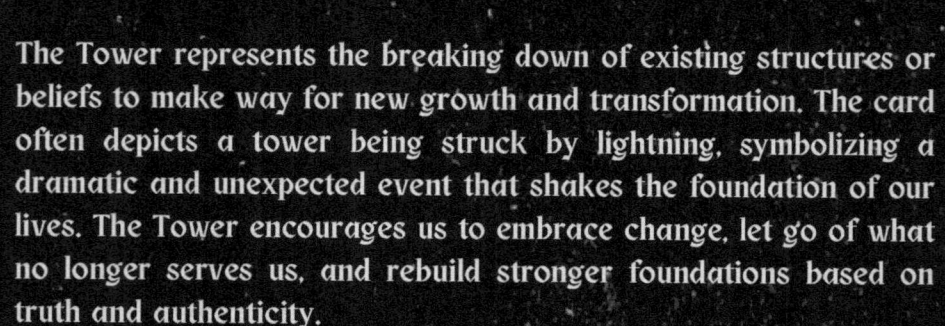

The Tower represents the breaking down of existing structures or beliefs to make way for new growth and transformation. The card often depicts a tower being struck by lightning, symbolizing a dramatic and unexpected event that shakes the foundation of our lives. The Tower encourages us to embrace change, let go of what no longer serves us, and rebuild stronger foundations based on truth and authenticity.

18

THE STAR

PROMPT

Create an artwork inspired by hope, inspiration, and guidance.

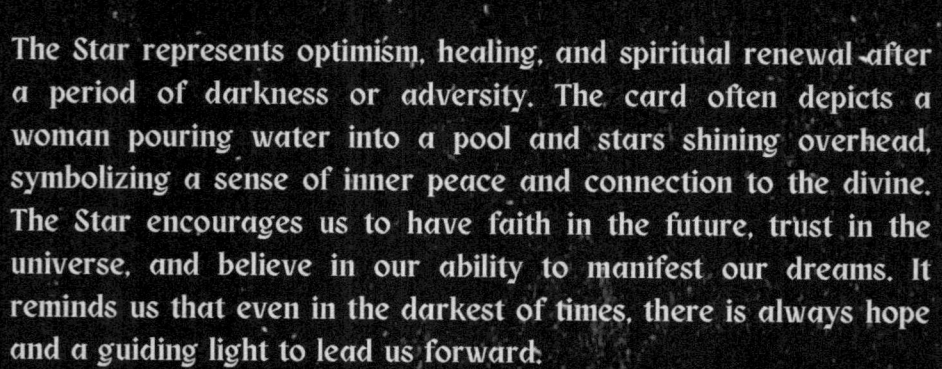

The Star represents optimism, healing, and spiritual renewal after a period of darkness or adversity. The card often depicts a woman pouring water into a pool and stars shining overhead, symbolizing a sense of inner peace and connection to the divine. The Star encourages us to have faith in the future, trust in the universe, and believe in our ability to manifest our dreams. It reminds us that even in the darkest of times, there is always hope and a guiding light to lead us forward.

19

THE MOON

PROMPT

Illustrate themes of illusion, intuition, and the subconscious mind.

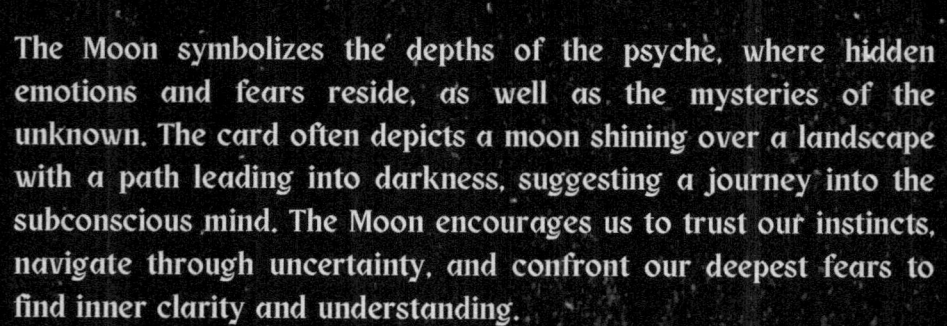

The Moon symbolizes the depths of the psyche, where hidden emotions and fears reside, as well as the mysteries of the unknown. The card often depicts a moon shining over a landscape with a path leading into darkness, suggesting a journey into the subconscious mind. The Moon encourages us to trust our instincts, navigate through uncertainty, and confront our deepest fears to find inner clarity and understanding.

20

THE SUN

PROMPT

Depict joy, vitality, and success in your artwork.

The Sun represents clarity, optimism, and enlightenment, bringing warmth and light to dispel darkness. The card often depicts a bright sun shining over a joyful scene, symbolizing a time of abundance, happiness, and fulfillment. The Sun encourages us to embrace positivity, express our true selves, and bask in the light of life's blessings.

21

JUDGMENT

PROMPT

Explore themes of rebirth, redemption, and self-reflection.

The Judgment symbolizes a time of reflection and transformation, where we are called to review our past actions, make amends, and embrace new beginnings. The card often depicts figures rising from graves, signifying a spiritual awakening or renewal of purpose. Judgment encourages us to take responsibility for our choices, release guilt or regret, and embrace the opportunity for personal growth and spiritual evolution.

22

THE WORLD

PROMPT

Create an artwork that symbolizes completion, fulfillment, and unity.

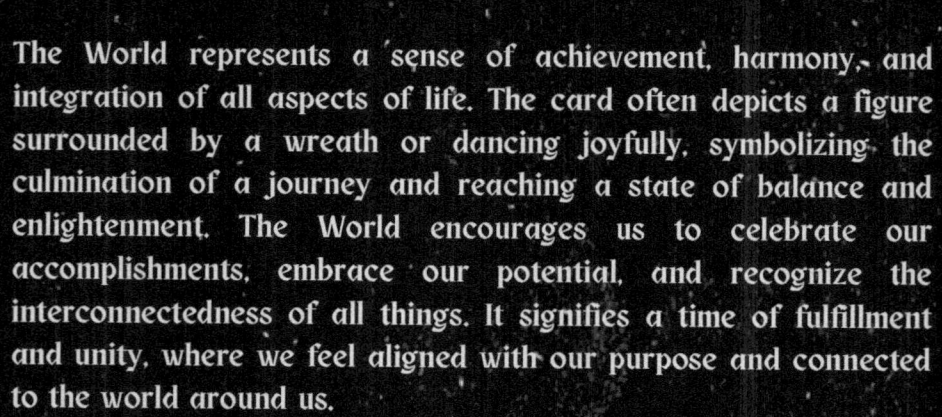

The World represents a sense of achievement, harmony, and integration of all aspects of life. The card often depicts a figure surrounded by a wreath or dancing joyfully, symbolizing the culmination of a journey and reaching a state of balance and enlightenment. The World encourages us to celebrate our accomplishments, embrace our potential, and recognize the interconnectedness of all things. It signifies a time of fulfillment and unity, where we feel aligned with our purpose and connected to the world around us.

23

ACES

PROMPT

Illustrate the essence of each suit's Ace card
(Wands, Cups, Swords, Pentacles).

The Aces in tarot represent the purest form of their respective suit's energy, signifying new beginnings, potential, and opportunity. Each Ace symbolizes the essence of its element:
Wands: Creativity, inspiration, and passion.
Cups: Emotions, intuition, and love.
Swords: Clarity, truth, and mental clarity.
Pentacles: Material abundance, prosperity, and practicality.

24

THE COURT

PROMPT

Create an artwork inspired by the personalities and archetypes of the court cards (Pages, Knights, Queens, Kings).

Page: Represents youth, curiosity, and new beginnings. Pages often signify a messenger or bearer of news.
Knight: Symbolizes action, ambition, and determination. Knights represent movement, adventure, and pursuit of goals.
Queen: Represents maturity, nurturing, and intuition. Queens embody compassion, wisdom, and emotional intelligence.
King: Symbolizes authority, leadership, and mastery. Kings represent strength, responsibility, and control.

Each Court Card can represent an individual in our lives or aspects of our personality. They offer insights into different qualities and roles we may need to embody or interact with in various situations.

25

IN SPIRITS

PROMPT

Make four illustrations each portraying different spirits of one element (Earth, Air, Fire, Water), and embodying their significance

Elemental spirits are sometimes invoked in rituals or spiritual practices for various purposes, such as protection, healing, or manifestation. They are also found in folklore, mythology, and esoteric teachings across cultures, each with their own interpretations and characteristics.

EARTH

Gnomes: Earth spirits depicted as small, stout creatures who dwell underground and are guardians of treasure or natural resources.
Dwarves: Earth spirits known for their craftsmanship and skill in metalworking, often portrayed as living deep within mountains.
Elves: Earth spirits associated with forests and nature, depicted as ethereal beings who protect wildlife and the natural world.

AIR

Sylphs: Air spirits depicted as airy beings, sometimes resembling humans with translucent wings, and are associated with the wind and clouds.
Fairies: Air spirits known for their mischievous nature and ability to move swiftly through the air, often depicted as tiny winged creatures.
Harpies: Air spirits depicted as bird-like creatures with the face of a woman, associated with storms and wind currents.

FIRE

Salamanders: Fire spirits often depicted as lizard-like creatures associated with flames and intense heat, believed to dwell in volcanoes and fiery environments.
Phoenix: Fire spirits symbolizing rebirth and renewal, depicted as a bird engulfed in flames that rises from its ashes.
Ifrits: Fire spirits from Middle Eastern folklore, known for their fiery temperament and association with desert landscapes.

WATER

Undines: Water spirits associated with bodies of water, such as rivers, lakes, and oceans, depicted as graceful female beings with the ability to control water.
Nymphs: Water spirits often depicted as beautiful maidens who inhabit natural water sources like streams, springs, and fountains.
Mermaids: Water spirits with the upper body of a human and the lower body of a fish, associated with the sea and maritime lore.

I hope this project brings you joy, inspiration, and perhaps a few moments of escape from the everyday

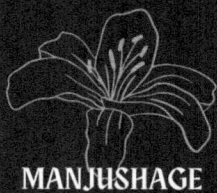

MANJUSHAGE

www.ingramcontent.com/pod-product-compliance
Lightning Source LLC
Chambersburg PA
CBHW070418230526
45471CB00006B/2863